FBC
2-
11/19
Sports

D1532329

BEDSIDE RACING

ABOUT THE AUTHOR

Willie Carson, four times champion jockey, was born in Stirling, Scotland in 1942 and began his racing career in 1959. His best year to date was 1978, when he rode 182 winners. He has won the Derby twice, on Troy (1979) and Henbit (1980). Off the track, he appears regularly on television, often in the BBC1 programme **A Question of Sport**.

WILLIE CARSON
BEDSIDE RACING

Illustrations by Martin Honeysett

Fontana
Collins

First published in Great Britain 1982
by J M Dent & Sons Ltd
Aldine House, 33 Welbeck Street, London W1

First issued in Fontana Paperbacks 1983

Copyright © Willie Carson 1982
Illustrations Copyright © Martin Honeysett 1982

Made by Lennard Books, Mackerye End,
Harpenden, Herts AL5 5DR

Editor Michael Leitch
Designed by David Pocknell's Company Ltd
Production Reynolds Clark Associates Ltd

CONDITIONS OF SALE
This book is sold subject to the condition
that it shall not, by way of trade or otherwise
be lent, re-sold, hired out or otherwise
circulated without the publisher's prior
consent in any form of binding or cover
than that in which it is published
: and without a similar condition
including this condition being imposed
on the subsequent purchaser

Printed and bound in Great Britain by
Collins, Glasgow

CONTENTS

PREFACE

I owe my career to a rhyme and a movie. The rhyme came first. I can't recall who started it, but it seemed to take hold so people would repeat it. When visitors came to the house, I'd be brought forward. Cue for the rhyme:

> 'Oh! (it began). You're so weee,
> Y'ought to be a jockeeee.'

I'm sure they meant well, but despite my size nothing was further from my mind than horses and racing. If I gave much thought to the future, I could vaguely see myself becoming a chef or carpenter. Until the movie. The movie was a racetrack saga called *Rainbow Jacket*. By the time I came out in the street afterwards, my daydreams had turned a decisive corner. In them I was now the boy in the film – just as well, if they ever want to do a sequel, since I hear the original actor is now six foot three; even taller than Lester.

In between daydreams I took riding lessons, finished school, and was accepted as an apprentice lad at Middleham, the famous Yorkshire stable of Captain Gerald Armstrong. There I was converted from a Saturday morning pony-clubber into a professional race-rider, a process rather like joining the Foreign Legion to escape from the Boy Scouts. In this book I have set down just some of the odd things that have happened to me and my friends in the racing game since those apprentice days. Nearly all of them, give or take a coat of varnish, are true; or so I believe. As you've probably found out, though, in this game there are few certainties.

A SUITABLE PLACE TO START

'Right,' said the eldest boy, 'tonight we'll do boxing.' Before any of the dozen of us had time even to think of protesting, let alone find the courage or words to do it, he began pairing us off. 'You against you. You against you. You . . .'

I was matched with Swindells. By most people's standards all the apprentices in that room were small. But by *my* standards Swindells was enormous. He was broad across the shoulders, had huge hands, plus a reputation as a slugger. I had been at Middleham long enough to appreciate that these lads didn't fool about when it came to boxing. Bare-knuckle fisticuffs was a traditional form of leisure in racing – a tradition that extends to an annual championship (with the gloves on) run at that time by the Anglo-American Sporting Club and staged in the plush and cigar-smoke of the London Hilton. As I well knew, when it came to boxing, these lads went at it like steam-hammers; blood ran as naturally as water.

In the minutes before it was my turn, the conviction overcame me that I would rather be a failed jockey than a doomed flyweight. I would take one and go down. But it would have to look convincing, or life would not have been worth living, even as a cripple. So for the opening moments of the fight I fizzed about, bright-eyed and keen, all fists, feet and elbows, even led a few punches. When I thought I was looking good, but maybe not quite good enough, I stuck out the jaw. Over came the haymaker. Someone counted me out.

So much for the frivolous side of life at Middleham, where I began my apprenticeship at the age of sixteen. The guide-books don't have much to say about Middleham: 'Wensleydale village with ruined castle, dismantled in 1646 . . . market place surrounded by Georgian houses . . . well-known as a centre for training race-horses.' The reality, if you look on the map, is that Middleham stands beside the biggest empty space in England. Out there to the south and west is miles and miles of . . . nothing. In dark moments I consoled myself that there could be no better place to start than on this Edge of Nowhere. The next place *had* to be better.

The Armstrong stables were a couple of miles out of the village. They truly conformed to the popular image of racing stables – bleak, dour, 'slightly up from Borstal', as more than one reflective racing man has put it. Boarding schools of the sterner kind operate on similar principles. Work, work, and more work – and whatever happens, don't let the little devils sneak off and have a rest, it only leads to Trouble. Certainly, the only time I sneaked off for an afternoon sleep and got caught, I received a whacking sound enough to keep me awake for the rest of the day.

The core of my life in those first years was the dunghill. Each morning at dawn, small sleepy apprentices struggled to balance overlong forks as they tackled the necessary ritual of mucking-out. With a sheet spread on the ground in front of the stable door, they charged the muck, loaded the fork, swung it back and dumped the load on the sheet. Then back into the muck. The art was to do it in one, clearing the stable floor so that only one journey was needed to the dunghill. This meant a more than full sheet, and was no simple task. You'd fold over one edge of the sheet, then the others in turn, reach down from no great height and gather the corners. Ready for transport. So: draw a big breath, twist, heave, and up on to the back, stagger sideways to check the balance, and off in the straightest possible line to the steaming mound in the middle of the yard. If any readers are thinking of taking this up as a hobby, there's one more thing you should know. Don't put the loose stuff on the bottom of the sheet; it finds its way through and runs down your back!

9

The Toe-Bite

Dunghills work very well as sauna baths. A bit on the primitive side, I would agree, but there's many a young apprentice who found himself being hoisted through a hole in the top, then covered up to the neck in steaming dung with orders not to move for the next half-hour.

Initiation was more the name of the game than slimming, but if you didn't have a head for heights it was just slightly better than the hay-sack ordeal. This alternative load of

fun involved the victim being tied with hay cord and strung up on the wall. Your prison was a hay sack, and the other lads would pass the cord through an iron loop in the wall, which acted as a pulley. And there you were left, three feet off the ground, to meditate on the wisdom of choosing a career in horseracing.

The apprentice years are not so spartan now. Today's beginner might get away with a hosing-down in ice-cold water, with repeat soakings every birthday, but a few years back there was a definite feudal system among the lads. No novice would be so daft as to get too near the bigger lads if he could help it. 'What, nothing to do? Grease my horse's feet then. And quick about it!'

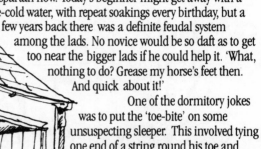

One of the dormitory jokes was to put the 'toe-bite' on some unsuspecting sleeper. This involved tying one end of a string round his toe and fixing the other end to a bed-post. If you allowed enough slack, nothing would happen until the morning. Then he'd wake up, push back the covers and try to jump out of bed. 'Aaarrgh!'

Egg Sandwiches

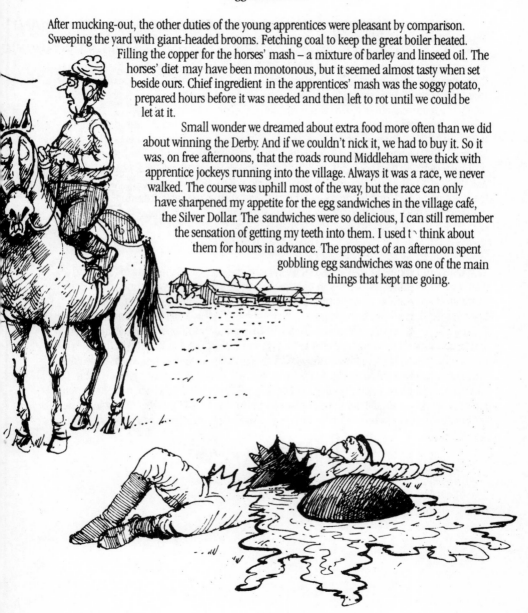

After mucking-out, the other duties of the young apprentices were pleasant by comparison. Sweeping the yard with giant-headed brooms. Fetching coal to keep the great boiler heated. Filling the copper for the horses' mash – a mixture of barley and linseed oil. The horses' diet may have been monotonous, but it seemed almost tasty when set beside ours. Chief ingredient in the apprentices' mash was the soggy potato, prepared hours before it was needed and then left to rot until we could be let at it.

Small wonder we dreamed about extra food more often than we did about winning the Derby. And if we couldn't nick it, we had to buy it. So it was, on free afternoons, that the roads round Middleham were thick with apprentice jockeys running into the village. Always it was a race, we never walked. The course was uphill most of the way, but the race can only have sharpened my appetite for the egg sandwiches in the village café, the Silver Dollar. The sandwiches were so delicious, I can still remember the sensation of getting my teeth into them. I used to think about them for hours in advance. The prospect of an afternoon spent gobbling egg sandwiches was one of the main things that kept me going.

Eating can be a dangerous game for jockeys, though the problem of 'making the weight' usually comes later in life. For many apprentices in their late teens the fear is that, no matter what they do, however little or much they eat, they will suddenly sprout. Huge hands and feet begin to appear on the ends of limbs no thicker than cornstalks. Then the limbs themselves get bigger, followed by the trunk that joins them, until the product is an Incredible Hulk, totally unsuited to race-riding. I was spared such problems. For me the problem with food was getting enough of it. Drink, though, was a different matter.

The pubs in the area were barred to us, so the first drink was taken outside, brought round the back by some understanding friend – or stranger, anyone would do. Alcohol works fast inside the slender frame of the apprentice jockey, and by the end of the first drink I'd feel strong enough and bold enough to go inside and order my own. If I was really lucky, I'd get that down and be into the third before the long arm of the landlord intervened, taking me by the scruff of the neck and lifting me out the door. Rarely was there any ill-feeling between customer and host – after three drinks I was gone anyway!

Love on the Bricks

At Middleham I started to go courting. It wasn't easy, the main obstacle being to find a girl who wasn't more than a foot taller than I was. Also there was a lot of competition from other apprentices with similar needs, similar problems. When, eventually, girls were found, we had to go to special lengths to keep them interested. My solution was to get to the venue, say a dance-hall, before anyone else, and fix myself a small pile of bricks behind the building. Of course, it was never as straightforward as it may sound to suggest a quiet stroll in the moonlight, then get her walking in the right direction, then remember just where I'd left the bricks, and finally manoeuvre her into position before the invisible mounting-block. Alan Ladd, so they say, had much the same trouble with tall leading ladies, as when Sophia Loren had to be sunk in a sandpit for the clinch scenes in **Boy on a Dolphin**. He was just lucky he didn't have to make his movies in the puddles and pitch dark at the back of a Yorkshire dance-hall!

MAN OVER HORSE

When you join a stable as an apprentice lad, your main task is to keep the horses in good condition. Horse maintenance, if you like. After a while, you are given a particular horse and become responsible for that animal's daily care. Then your masters decide to turn you into a jockey, and you find yourself learning a quite different trade. The common factor, in the early months at least, is that you don't really know what you are doing. And if ever an animal can sense this, it's a horse.

At Middleham, where I began, the first horse entrusted to me was a mare called Marija. She must have taken one look at Carson W. and decided: here's a greenhorn who needs sorting out. She waited until I was nervously applying grease to her rear hooves, then kicked out. 'Not like that, you fool,' was probably all she meant to say; but the kick, however playful, hurt.

Another of Marija's games was to stand up in the corner of her box when I went in to catch her, and put her backside to me. Whichever side of her I tried to go, she'd swivel so I couldn't get near her. The head lad knew what to do: he'd come along and give a sharp growl. This brought her head round and he'd grab it. But when I tried that . . . no way. Her eyes – or rather the one eye that I could see – gleamed in the darkness of the box. 'You're not catching me,' was its mischievous message.

In the end you learn how to look after horses and ride them, and then the time comes, all being well, to learn the arts of race-riding. It's a long haul, and, here again, the horses don't always co-operate. My first win would have made a good Disney cartoon. I was riding Pinkers Pond. He was so lively it was a real wrestling match just to get him down to the start. Then we were off, and all Pinkers Pond seemed to want was to get back in his box as quickly as possible. We started like a rocket, with me hanging on behind, my body parallel with the horse's back, arms coming out of their sockets. Precise details of the next few minutes are beyond me. Suffice to say, Pinkers Pond ripped up the opposition, and I came home a bewildered hero.

Clicks and Raspberries

Unfortunately, as I learned, there is more to race-riding than being towed round at the fastest rate of knots. Some horses have little wish to give of their all, and the nub of the problem becomes: how do you make them go faster?

Clicking with the tongue is universal. It's still used for training horses on the long rein, and they associate it with the command: Go! It can also work on the race track, but it isn't all that loud, and in the din and chaos of a race may get lost.

Shouting and screaming is a better bet. Or raspberries. A good crisp raspberry, delivered just behind the horse's ear, can startle the horse enough to make him shoot forward. He doesn't like it, but it works. In one race, over a mile and a half, the jockey blasted his horse into the lead and kept up a spray of rude noises all the way round. Every time another horse challenged, the jockey peppered his mount with another salvo. It won. Later, when the press gathered round to ask him how he'd got on, the jockey said:

'Oh, farted in!'

The remark did not appear in the next day's papers!

Of course, you can let the magic slip away if you aren't careful. One four-horse race, I thought the main rival wouldn't be too difficult. I got in behind; my horse was one that responded to yelling and screaming, so I started the barrage. His ears went back, and off we went, past the opposition. I had the race won. But once I'd hit the front, I forgot about the yelling and screaming and just got on with my job. Yards before the line, this other horse steamed up – Whooosh! – went by and beat me.

17

The Stick

One thing a lot of horses definitely don't like is the stick. Used skilfully, the stick can push a horse to its racing limits. But if it doesn't respond, there's no point in just whacking away. The stick is not there for punishing the horse, and should always be used with care.

Some of the strangest moments in racing occur when jockeys take their sticks to each other. No-one who saw it will ever forget Brian Connortown and Taffy Thomas duelling with their sticks as they crossed the line.

Lester Piggott starred in another famous incident, at Deauville. Alain Lequeux was leading Lester, but only just. Lester, however, had lost his stick. Not only that, he knew he was on a very lazy horse which needed a lot of encouragement. Up ahead, Lequeux was waving away with his stick. So Lester began to get in rhythm with him, then he glided alongside – and took the stick off him! He did it beautifully, as if the whole movement had been rehearsed for days. There was no snatching or fighting, it was the coolest heist ever seen on a race track.

The crowd at Deauville loved it, and the video replay was shown and shown umpteen times. The stewards weren't so keen, though; Lester got 28 days' suspension.

When I saw Lester a little while later, I asked him what he'd been doing. He said:

'I asked him for it.'

'You what?' I said. 'You asked him for it? You can't speak French.'

'I said: "Le bâton, s'il vous plaît." '

Later, Lester also claimed to have offered the stick back to Lequeux when the horses had passed the post and were pulling up, but – 'He wouldn't have it,' said Lester in his extraordinary deadpan style.

The Chief Barker

Another way to make your horse go faster is to disconcert the opposition so much that they can't race. This brings us, inevitably, to The Barker, also known as Greville Starkey. His terrier bark has been heard on and off race courses for twenty years.

At an airport check-in desk, Greville put up his bag. 'Ruff ruff!' said the bag. 'Shurrup,' snarled Greville at the hump of the canvas on the desk.

The girl on the desk appeared to take no notice at first. But Greville persisted. 'Ruff ruff!'

'Shurrup, will you!' A Starkey elbow is raised in anger at the bag.

'Ruff.'

'Shut that! SITT! Good boy.'

But the barking would not stop, and as the girl leaned anxiously forward to look at the source of the noise, Greville put the bag down on the floor, cursed it briefly and booted it clean across the hallway.

'Aaagh!' screamed the girl.

Another time, Greville went with a group to Argentina. There he almost met his match. He was doing his dog noises in the usual places likely to cause most embarrassment – hotel lifts, restaurants, inside locked toilets – when he came upon a rival. This rival would follow Greville's bark by a hard slapping noise and a bout of the most pathetic howling any of us had ever heard. Greville and the other feller, a European living in Argentina, had the makings of a great man-dog team. A pity there isn't more demand for that kind of thing . . . .

Staying On

When you're balanced in mid-air somewhere above the saddle of a racehorse travelling at 40 mph, in minimum contact with the animal, the difference between finishing the course and taking a bone-cracking header can be fine indeed. For me the supreme illustration of this happened with Dibidale in the Oaks.

She was a big filly, very deep-bodied. Before the race all the usual checks were made, but this time something went wrong. As we came round Tattenham Corner, the girth came loose and the saddle started slipping back. As I realized what was happening, I could feel the reins getting longer and longer; the saddle was askew, there was nothing to hold it on, I was losing my balance and within seconds of hitting the deck. It was true Wild West stuff. How can Willie Carson – bound and gagged in the blazing boxcar as it hurtles towards the edge of the ravine – escape?

I edged my feet out of the irons till just the toes were in contact. Now I was hanging on to Dibidale's mane rather than the reins, and my hindquarters, drifting ever backwards, were about parallel with the horse's and slewing sideways.

At the last moment I gritted my teeth, leaped forward, abandoning the saddle, and landed on the horse's back. Incredibly, there was still time to ride a finish. A quick sprint later, we passed the post in third position.

The crowd, who'd seen it all happening, gave a special cheer and, all in all, I thought the horse and I had done pretty well. But the judges, correctly, disqualified us. Not because of the bareback finish, but because the leadcloth, which made up my weight to the necessary 9

stone, had fallen off when the saddle slipped round to the horse's belly. So, after the race, I didn't weigh in correctly. If I'd been heavier, and not needed a leadcloth, I'd have been third. How's that for small consolation?

The Pacemaker

In France for a Sunday meeting. I was down for a mile-and-a-quarter race on a horse called Ksar. The horse to beat was Admetus, but it wasn't as simple as that. The wily French stable had another runner in the race, ridden by an apprentice and bound to be given the role of pacemaker. Oddly, my pale-blue colours were fairly similar to the rival pair, which gave me something to think about.

We jumped off, and the apprentice took the early lead I had expected. I sat second, and waited. At about the halfway point the pacemaker was still going well, and I began to wonder if we couldn't encourage him to do a little more. Admetus was back in the field, but still in touch.

I got up close to the pacemaker and shouted, in my best French:

'Allez! Allez vite!'

The apprentice looked round quickly. Had there been a change of plan? He saw my pale-blue colours and must have thought so. He asked his horse, and the horse responded. Away they went, with me in pursuit. This left Admetus going further and further adrift, and me with a great chance to attack the pacemaker when he began to tire. But for me the biggest kick was imagining the rage of the French jockeys, not to mention the apoplectic owner in the grandstand. 'Sacre bleu!' 'Zat perfidious Carson!' Definitely one up for Britain.

Weak End in Brighton

There are certainly times when you don't want to make *all* the running. One day I was going down to Brighton in the train with trainer Bernard van Cutsem. We were pretty confident that our horse would win easily, but it would be better in the long term if he didn't win *too* easily. The Morland Brewery race was coming up, and the weights for it had not yet been compiled. No need to overdo things.

Trouble was, the horse had the race to himself, and with half a furlong to go there wasn't anyone else in it. So I eased him down while the others did a bit of running. Too much, as it turned out. The opposition came belting up and as we crossed the line it wasn't clear whether I had won or been nosed out of it. Photo-finish. I cantered on. It was my first outing after a suspension, so I took a long, long time to pull up while they got the photograph ready.

I came back slowly, listening for my number, squinting down to check that what I thought was my number was the same as the number on the horse. Seconds ticked into minutes, and I could feel the long arm of the stewards reaching out for my neck once more. Then came the verdict: me, by a short head. The long arm of the stewards slid noiselessly back into its socket – an invisible warning, but one I would remember.

Master Plan

Bernard van Cutsem could also produce the telling statement when the occasion demanded Surrounded by newspapermen after his horse had won a top handicap at Royal Ascot, he was asked:

> 'Mr van Cutsem, what are your plans for this horse?'
> 'Dear boy,' he answered, 'that *was* the plan!'

A GREAT LITTLE RACECOURSE

If some tracks have passed their best, others have never had a best they'd notice losing. Nostalgia for greater days is not in their book. They are moved only by some faintly sensed urge that it is better to survive than close their battered gates for ever.

Jockeys, being a highly perceptive, intelligent body of men, are usually among the first to detect that a track and its facilities are not all they might be. Among the signs, noted in a flash by their quivering professional antennae, are:

The changing room has one nail or less per man for hanging clothes.

FIRST ONE INTO THE CHANGING ROOM GETS TO USE THE NAIL.

The lone shower sends out red-hot needles of water than no-one can get near. The flow continues until the end of the third race, then the shower packs up altogether.

The grandstand would, as the estate agents say, benefit from renovation.

HERE'S ANOTHER ONE WANTS TO GET SOME PRACTICE IN FOR THE RACE

Some of the bends are extraordinarily tight, especially the Wall of Death, as it is known locally. It's a tight right turn, three furlongs from home. If you go wide and miss it, you're out running against the buses.

There are four people around the winner's enclosure to clap you when you come in.
The prize-money is not just small, it is rather less than the apprentices' minimum wage.

SAUNA REVELS

Weight is a perennial problem for jockeys, and the sauna is one of the best ways to shed a few quick pounds. But you can have too much of a good thing, as John Gorton will readily testify.

The meeting that day was at Newbury. It was towards the end of the season, when jockeys tend to be a little more light-hearted than usual. For John Gorton it was a very special day, too – his last day of riding in the UK; afterwards he was going back to South Africa to be a trainer. He was staying down at Jimmy Lindley's place for the Friday-Saturday meeting; and Greville Starkey was there too.

They were in the sauna on the Saturday morning, getting weight off for the afternoon races. It can get boring, spending hours in the sauna day after day. So, to liven things up a bit, Greville went out and locked the door, leaving John trapped inside. The heat was by then pretty intense and John, though a good sweater, was really panting. He pounded and pounded on the door. In vain. The house might have been deserted.

'Give me a drink,' he pleaded at last. 'If you won't let me out, at least give me a drink.'

'Right, hang on, John,' said a voice promptly, and one of his captors fetched a bottle of champagne.

Just near the foot of the door was a small grille. They stuck a straw in the bottle, and bent the other end through the grille. John was instantly down on his knees, sucking at the straw. As the others watched with quiet satisfaction, the level of the champagne went steadily down. This proved at least that John had not lost any of his main faculties, so they kept him in a little bit longer. The heat grew no easier, and John carried on taking the occasional draught.

When, at last, they let him out, John was burning. He dashed out into the garden and flung himself screaming into Jimmy Lindley's pond – not the cleanest and sweetest of ponds, but John didn't care. 'Aaaaaah!!' In he went.

At the races, John was in excellent form, though not for racing. His body had cooled off, but the champagne was still doing its work. Fortunately, the co-operative spirit among jockeys was at its finest. Tenderly, they guided John down to the start, ushered him into the stalls, and propped him up in the saddle when his concentration seemed to wander.

The actual rides weren't the best of John's career. But at least he got home safely, and with most of his dignity intact was able to retire from the British scene – and from taking saunas at Jimmy Lindley's!

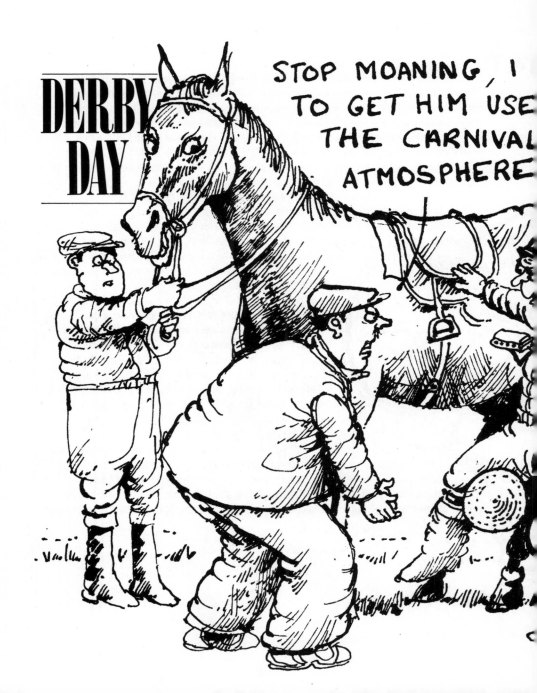

No other race rouses a jockey like the Derby. It is, simply, the most special race in the calendar. The preparations, looking ahead to the great day, begin months ahead – almost before the end of the previous flat season. You're not actually worrying about it, but all the same if you're a trainer and you've got a champion two year-old that looks like staying a mile and a half, you think about it a long way ahead, planning where he should run before the Derby, what kind of build-up you should give him.

For the jockey the worry, the real apprehension, starts about a week before the race. If you're on a fancied horse, you start dreaming about how you're going to do. You have the same dream maybe fifty times – and it helps a lot if you can win forty-nine of them!

Then comes the day. It starts just like any other. Wednesday morning. Ride-work. Then, after ride-work, it becomes a different day. You have to set off two hours earlier than usual to get to the track in good time. (The Derby is also the only race in the calendar for which you take two horse-boxes for one horse – in case the leading box breaks down.) By the time you arrive, the sense of urgency has got to you. The traffic has been nose to tail for what seemed like a hundred miles, and on the track some kind of mad carnival is going on.

Derby Day has been a state as well as a great public occasion for more than a century. In 1848, in the days of Lord George Bentinck, the 'Napoleon of the Turf', the House of Commons voted by 103 to 90 to knock off for the day, so that MPs who wished to might join the 15,000 to 20,000 crowds who surged towards Epsom Downs on that magic Wednesday. The holiday atmosphere has been celebrated by squadrons of writers and painters. But what do the horses think about it?

Surprisingly little has been recorded about how the horses cope with all the uproar. One man with first-hand knowledge was Rufus Beasley. In his autobiography, published privately, he recalled preparing Bounteous for the 1961 Derby. The first thing Beasley did was hire a brass band! The trumpeters and trombonists lined his private Moulton gallops and blasted away as the colt passed them. This was done to ensure that the fairground din at Epsom would make Bounteous – and his jockey – feel quite at home.

I have never had the benefit of musical practice before the day – not even with so much as a string quartet. But I do know that for a jockey the adrenaline starts to run as soon as you get to Epsom. The first two races are OK, mainly because they give you something to do (you can even enjoy them!). Then the clock ticks ever so slowly round towards three.

In the weighing room the noisy ones go quiet, the quiet ones start chattering. If you're on a fancied runner, there is enormous tension. Everyone in that room wants to be first past the stick, and the more they think about it, the more screwed up they can get. Out on the course, that's the big trap. You want to do well so badly, you can try too hard and make mistakes.

It can work the other way. You think you can't possibly win, then something happens. In 1979, I was on Troy. I'd got myself in behind Edward Hide on Lasko Floko – a great big hulk of a horse. I couldn't get by him and he was taking me back. When I did find a way past, I had nowhere to go so I stayed inside and waited till we got into the turn. From the six- to the five-furlong markers I remember thinking, 'Ah well, never mind. There's always next year.' Then suddenly Troy started to give a bit more. I took him out, and Whooosh!

You could say that if we hadn't been in trouble earlier, we'd never have won. Troy had only found this late strength because I hadn't been bothering him all through. Earlier on, I *had* been pushing at him, but nothing had happened, so I decided, 'It's no good. Try again next year.' I left him alone for a furlong and a half, and then all of a sudden I could *feel* the power in him.

The start had been very fast and he'd no doubt needed a breather. That was when he hadn't responded. But now he'd got his lungs filled up with oxygen. He'd got his wind back … and off we went.

We came home by eight lengths. Afterwards, although it was my first Derby win, I took it fairly calmly, to begin with. All the clamour, the pats on the back, the interviews. I was very elated, enjoying it all, but there was no real feeling I'd achieved anything extra special. That evening we all went out to dinner in London; same restaurant as usual, same people. The only difference was, this time I paid the bill! But still it hadn't sunk in. Not even when I went off to the hotel, got into bed and fell asleep.

Halfway through the night, I woke up. A man possessed, at last, I rose up in bed, eyes wide open, and shouted: 'I've won the Derby!!!' Then fell back and went to sleep again.

HOW OLD IS A JOCKEY?

Put another way, when is a jockey in his prime? A young jockey, or someone who doesn't know the first thing about race-riding, might say: 'When age and experience blend best,' or some such pomposity. Then try asking an older, wiser jockey if he agreed. 'Get out,' he'd say. 'That's when he ought to retire!'

One thing is certain. There is no lower age limit, just as there is nothing to stop you cracking your bones until all they leave is dustmarks on the grass. According to the *Guinness Book of*

YOU TRY TELLING HIM HE'S GETTING PAST IT

Records, Frank Wootton (1893–1940) rode his first winner in South Africa when he was 9 years 10 months. At the other end of the age scale, the *Guinness* recordbreaker is the American jockey Levi Burlingame, who rode his last race at Stafford, Kansas, in 1932 at the age of 80.

In his autobiography, the trainer Rufus Beasley makes claims for his father, Harry Beasley, that would put him well in the vanguard of the ancients. Some other highlights of Harry Beasley's career are also worth a second look. Apparently, he rode in 13 Grand Nationals between 1879 and 1892, won once, in 1891, and finished second three times. He won a race at Punchestown when he was 71, and then, to crown a lifetime of living dangerously, rode in a flat race at Ballydoyle when he was 84! I can't verify this last feat, but I can, if necessary, produce an eye-witness who swears he saw Harry Beasley ride at the Curragh when he was 80 years old.

Of course, it's all very well to be old and still in the game, and secretly pleased with yourself for lasting so long, but maybe it's not so good for trade if *too many* people know how old you are. 'Not laying my money on that old skeleton,' punters might say in their blunt fashion, and a time could soon come when your odds never seem to drop below 66–1.

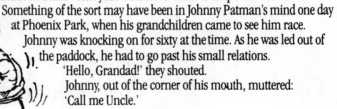

Something of the sort may have been in Johnny Patman's mind one day at Phoenix Park, when his grandchildren came to see him race.

Johnny was knocking on for sixty at the time. As he was led out of the paddock, he had to go past his small relations.

'Hello, Grandad!' they shouted.

Johnny, out of the corner of his mouth, muttered: 'Call me Uncle.'

THE OWNER

The simple pleasure that every owner takes in victory shone on the face of Frank Woodhouse as his horse came to the last, three lengths clear. He beamed, he rubbed his hands. The horse, knowing nothing of this, cannoned into the hurdle and nosedived. Up in the stands, Frank collapsed.

'Get him a whiskey,' someone cried.

Frank managed to raise his head. 'Make it a double,' he croaked.

This simple urge to own winners may not always coincide with the deeper strategies of the trainer. He may have something up his sleeve – and for the time being is content to keep it there. As one trainer said to another: 'Owners should be treated like mushrooms. Keep them in the dark as long as you can, and well filled up with shit!'

IT'S NOT FAIR, HE GAVE THE HORSE *TWO* LUMPS.

Excuse Me, Your Lordship

Owners of racehorses are shrouded in a strange feudal atmosphere that goes back in time to the beginnings of the sport, when the nobility had exclusive charge of everything that went on. Things are a little different now, but to the young apprentice – hungry, underpaid, and all the other things that go with being at the bottom of the heap – the owner has something that is without compare. He has money. The more money he has, the more he is to be revered, like a kind of golden statue from which small nuggets can be chipped on racedays and visits to the stables.

Some handouts are traditional, amounts are eagerly discussed in advance, and comparisons made both before and after the event. Imagine, then, the creeping horror with which one stable lad watched as a particular lord patted the horse, put his hand in his pocket, drew out a sugar lump, gave it to the horse . . . and turned to go. The lad was so stunned, he couldn't stop himself from tugging heavily on his cap and saying:

'Excuse me, your Lordship.'

'Yes?'

'Er, well,' said the lad, giving the peak of his cap another pull; by now the top half of his face had disappeared, but distress registered plainly on the lower regions.

'Yes?' said his Lordship. 'What is it?'

'Well,' stumbled the lad. 'It's just that . . . what shall I tell the other lads you gave me?'

Vic Oliver claimed his horse was trained on whisky, rum and brandy. 'He wasn't the best horse in the race, but he was the happiest.'

Hitching a Ride

The gift of meanness is not at all exclusive to owners of racehorses. Some trainers have it too. In fact, there was an Irish trainer who may take the all-comers' prize when it comes to not opening the wallet. He would never, for instance, buy a railway ticket for a travelling lad when the horses went by train. One of his ex-apprentices, also Irish, has fond memories of having to smuggle himself in with the horses, and lie low for the whole of the journey.

'If a porter came round, you'd have to shift yourself and be out of sight up under the horse's belly. And when you got to the station, you had to jump out early then run along the platform and make as if you were meeting the train!

'Worst of all, though,' he said, 'he would never even buy you a drink!'

Taxi!

A sure sign of nerves in a jump-jockey is if he takes one hand off the reins as he jumps a fence. The loose arm shoots straight up in the air, as a way of keeping balance, and the manoeuvre is known among jockeys as 'calling for a cab'. It's the sort of thing guaranteed not to endear a jockey to the watching owner. Old Harry, now one of the grand veterans, remembers standing next to a nervous owner one day:

'The horse was odds-on favourite and this guvnor had a packet on him. But his jockey was getting the butterflies, and every time he came to a fence, up went the arm as if he was calling for a cab. Of course, it wasn't helping the horse much. In the end this guvnor looked down at me, just after the jockey'd taken another fence and done it again. He said:

' "I wish that bastard wouldn't keep waving me goodbye!" '

'I've Got Something For You'

Bonzo thought it must be his lucky day. His horse had won well, and he was leading him round, when he came across the owner, a quiet, slightly mysterious lady. She smiled encouragingly at Bonzo and leaned forward.

'I've got something for you,' she said.

'Oh, thank you very much, madam,' said Bonzo.

'Yes,' said the owner. 'I'll see you next time round.'

As Bonzo set off again, she pulled out an envelope. Bonzo thought to himself: 'Sound, here. Could be twenty-five in this.' Next time he came round, the owner slipped him the envelope.

'Here you are,' she said, 'and mind you look after it. It's precious.'

TO THE FINISH LINE —
AND HURRY

Bonzo couldn't wait to be by himself. He tore open the envelope. Inside was a photograph of the horse.

'By God,' said Bonzo later. 'I thought there was twenty-five quid in there, and it was a photograph. Cost me a fiver to have it framed!'

All For Glory

One owner was a bit slow in coming forward. Whenever a likely moment presented itself, I'd give him the expectant look and he'd say:

'Well, of course, you do it for the glory, really.'

I took this for a while, then I thought it was time to put my case a bit more strongly. Next time he tried to fob me off with his line about glory, I said to him:

'That's all very well, sir. But they won't buy that glory in Harrod's.'

I kept this up through the season. 'Well, sir, they won't buy glory in Harrod's.' At the end of the year he gave me . . . a gift voucher for Harrod's!

The Occasional Mistake

The race was the Bessborough Stakes at Royal Ascot, run over a mile and a half. I was riding Neltino for Lady Beaverbrook. The horse had won well on his last time out and was fancied for this race. We went quite fast to begin with, then I dropped him in on the rails behind Lester Piggott, who was also on a fancied horse. I followed him for six furlongs, and by then we were both in good positions. Lester was behind the leader and I was behind Lester, with the rest of the field around us.

Then, as we came towards the turn into the straight, the leading horse started to lose ground. As this happened, the rest of the field moved up past us. Every time Lester tried to get out and round the pacemaker he was knocked back in; I was trying to do the same, with the same result. We were boxed up.

By the time we came into the straight, I was virtually last, behind Lester, and from there the horse would have had to have been Concorde to catch the others and win. I'd left him with far too much to do, so I didn't press him and we finished nowhere. It was one of those things that happen. However, at Royal Ascot, the owner is certain to be there, and misfortune seems that much harder to bear.

In the next race I was also riding for Lady Beaverbrook. Well, I thought, there'll be long faces in the paddock, and maybe I'll get a telling-off. When I arrived, Lady Beaverbrook was talking to Sir Gordon Richards, her racing manager.

'Jockeys do make mistakes occasionally, don't they, Sir Gordon?' said Lady B.

'Yes, ma'am, they do,' replied Sir Gordon.

I decided my best move was to tell them what Lester had said to me after the race, when I had blamed him for getting me boxed in. I'd said:

'What the hell were you doing to me there? I was following you.'

Lester said: 'What do you want me to do, go *over* them?'

AND ON HIS HEADSTONE I WANT WRITTEN, 'BOXED IN AGAIN'.

STABLEMATES

Old Johnny was a great all-rounder, whose duties included driving the horsebox. After a good day at Redcar, he stopped awhile to celebrate, had one too many, perhaps, then walked back to the horsebox.

'Right lads,' he said. 'Let's go.'

Off he went again to the canteen, to get a cup of coffee before setting off. When he came back, he hooked up the ramp, climbed into the cab and set off back to the stables, an hour's drive away.

The trainer always met the horseboxes on their return. When Johnny drove in, he walked up.

'That was a good day.'

'Yes sir,' said Johnny. 'Two winners. Very good day.'

He bustled round to lower the ramp. He got it down, opened the box. No horses.

Trainer: 'Where are the horses, Johnny?'

Johnny: 'Think they must be at Redcar, sir!'

Taking a Breather

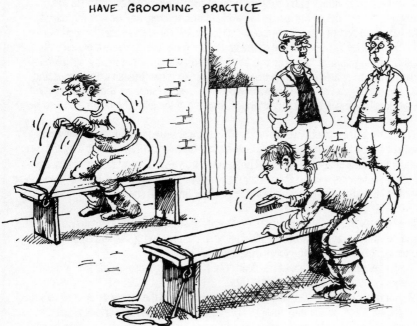

AND AFTER RIDING PRACTICE THEY HAVE GROOMING PRACTICE

One of the training devices when I was a lad involved a saddle, or a sack, a bench and a bridle. The trainer tied the bridle round the end of the bench, the apprentice sat down and took the reins.

The exercise was to push with the arms, up and back, maybe a hundred times. It was sweaty work, with the trainer constantly urging:

'Put some force into it, boy!'

Then the 'horse' would change its legs and start leading with the other one, so you'd have to change your arms round, without losing rhythm, then push, push, push – just as a boxer pounds at a punch-bag.

Ted Larkins was on the bench one day. He'd had a good go at it, then started to tire. The trainer was on to him:

'What's the matter, boy?'

Ted said: 'Just giving it a breather round the turn, sir!'

45

Chop-Chop

A stranger walked into a village pub on the Berkshire Downs one winter evening. He was a stranger not only to the village, but also to the world of horseracing, and he was surprised to find all the bar stools occupied by sharp-faced men in peaked caps whose legs dangled two feet clear of the floor. A lively log fire burned in the grate. The walls above it were crowded with framed colour photographs of horses and jockeys. The talk was all about racing, sprinkled with in-jokes and punctuated with loud laughter, and the stranger listened with interest and sipped his beer. It was good beer, the fire was welcoming, and the stranger thought to himself that if he stayed a bit longer, he too might understand one of the jokes. So he ordered another pint.

The talk was then about two year-olds. The stranger stared into his beer. Two years old seemed *very* young, he thought, even allowing that horses matured quickly. Why, that was just a matter of months after they were ... The stranger frowned. What were they called, the ones you saw on calendars, jolting about after their mothers on long spindly legs? As the elusive word at last came into view on the forefront of his brain, he cried:

'Foals!'

The bar talk froze. All heads turned to stare at the stranger. Feeling isolated and foolish, and not wishing to be discovered stiff in a ditch next morning, the stranger thought he had better explain himself to the short-legged group.

'It was hearing you talk about two year-olds. It seems very young, that's all. I mean, they've barely stopped being foals ... haven't they?'

The stranger looked around the weather-beaten faces of the men on the bar stools for some sign of understanding. He found none. The landlord, who had been drying glasses, put down his cloth and with a sideways glance at the stranger vanished through a curtain of red and yellow plastic tapes. Feeling more and more as though he, in the role of innocent traveller, had fallen among a cut-throat band, a modern version of those Devonshire brandy smugglers of the 19th century, the stranger plunged on:

'I mean, horses must have to, er, grow up very quickly to be out on the racecourse at the age of two ... mustn't they?'

More silence. More uncomprehending looks. Someone in a green quilted waistcoat blew a jet of cigar smoke into the base of a lamp shade, and watched it swirl about, his mouth hanging open, lower lip curled over. More silence. Then a man with a mauve nose and a clashing turquoise roll-neck sweater, who could have been Irish, said:

'Well, you see, sir, it's a quick life they have. The horses.' He went on: 'That's when they do their racing. When they're two and t'ree. After that they can retire, go out to stud. Sultans for the rest of their days . . . .'

'Ah, that's the good ones, the winners,' broke in a villainous-looking thin-faced man with long dark sideburns. 'The good ones go to stud. But the ones who don't win go for gelding. Fsssst!' He made a lightning pass through the air with one hand. 'Turns them into steeplechasers. That's the difference. Spend the rest of their days flogging round the jumps, while the top nobs live the life of Reilly.'

'I see,' said the stranger, rather shocked by this information. 'It seems, it seems a little severe,' he stammered. 'I mean, the penalty for not winning.' To himself he wondered how they did it; was there a special man you called in, a professional gelder? Fssssst!? He shuddered.

'Well, sir, it's very competitive, you see, the racing,' said the man who could have been Irish. 'There isn't room for them all out there on the flat.'

YOU HAVEN'T ... GELDED HIM?

'Yeah,' said the thin-faced man. 'Of course, if they knew . . . .' He paused.

'Yes?' said the stranger. He felt the conversation was taking a macabre turn, and was distinctly uneasy. 'Knew what?'

'Well, if they knew what was going to happen . . . .' continued the thin-faced man. He looked down at his beer mat, drew a long, wickedly sharp knife from his pocket and reflectively removed a slice from the top of his left thumb-nail. 'I've always thought,' he resumed, pointing his knife at the stranger for emphasis, 'that if they knew what was going to happen . . . then they'd run a bloody sight faster!'

This image, of a race in which a bunch of three year-olds flee the gelder's knife, went down well in the bar. Amid the general guffaws, no-one noticed that the stranger had fallen down in a dead faint.

Bonzo and the Guvnor

At Newmarket they had a lot of daft sayings going round at one time. One of these was:

'Have you seen them?'

'Seen who?'

'The Little Yellow Men.'

No-one knew what they were, just the Little Yellow Men. One day Bonzo was riding out with the other lads. They were going round a cinder track when someone said to Bonzo:

'Bet you wouldn't ask the Guvnor.'

'Ask him what?'

'About the Little Yellow Men.'

Bonzo wasn't all that keen. The Guvnor was a fierce character. He was supposed to be a bit deaf, too, which made him all the more touchy. Before Bonzo could stop him, though, the other feller yelled out the Guvnor's Christian name. Not at all deaf that day, and twice as irritable by the look of him, the Guvnor span round immediately.

'What?' he shouted, eyes narrowing, looking for trouble.

Too late for Bonzo to withdraw. Besides, he was on a dare, so he rode over to the Guvnor and said:

'Have you seen them?'

'Seen what?' glowered the Guvnor.

Bonzo, unfortunately, started laughing. Behind him, the other lads started laughing too.

'Seen what?' demanded the Guvnor. 'What have I seen?'

Eventually Bonzo managed to splutter: 'The Little Yellow Men.'

WE FEEL SORT OF RESPONSIBLE, SO WE'VE COME TO HELP YOU OUT.

The Guvnor went white. 'Ah, think you're a comedian, do you, my friend? Right, I'll see you later.' And stormed off.

The Guvnor must have had a word with the head lad, because when Bonzo had finished, and was quietly crossing the yard, planning to make himself scarce for the rest of the day, the head lad suddenly appeared.

'Come here, you,' he roared. Bonzo had no chance. He went over. 'Right. Been trying it on with the Guvnor, have you? Fancy yourself as a comedian? Right. I've got a job for you.'

'What's that?' asked Bonzo, edgily.

The head lad took Bonzo down to the paddock. It was in the days before that stable had an indoor ride, and the paddock was laid with a straw ring. The head lad pointed to the straw. He said:

'I want you to come down every afternoon and pick that up.'

So, every day, down went Bonzo to the paddock, picked up the heavy, sodden straw and put it in heaps for the muck-wagon. It took him a week before he was through. And every day, the Guvnor's missus used to come down to the paddock with her dogs. And every day she'd ask:

'Have you seen any yet?'

Call Yourself a Trainer?

Tempting though it may be to answer back, most lads keep their cool, or at least bottle their rage until the guvnor is out of sight. Answering back has this simple drawback: if you are a lad, you can never win. However, if you want to exit in a blaze of glory, and never work again, answering back has its satisfactions.

One lad had been getting rattier and rattier. He couldn't do a thing right, always copping it from the Old Man – unjustly, too, or so he thought. It all came to the boil one morning. The lad started answering back. At first the Old Man couldn't credit it, then he came back with a few blistering comments about the lad and his indifferent record in the stable. That did it. Suddenly the lad burst out:

'And do you call yourself a trainer? Call yourself a trainer? You couldn't train bloody roses to grow up a wall!'

He let go the horse he was holding, and a hundred thousand pounds worth of horseflesh went roaring off round the field. Seeing the horse running wild must have convinced the lad his days were numbered. He bolted for the gate, and hasn't been seen since!

The Guvnor's Wife

You've seen those Westerns where the cowboys chase each other through a patch of woodland. The one being chased ducks under a low branch, but his pursuer doesn't see it in time and the branch lifts him clean out of the saddle. You'd think the branch would break, wouldn't you? Well, mostly it does; but not always.

One day the Guvnor's wife – not she of the Little Yellow Men – was out riding through the woods down a narrow track. It was pouring with rain and very muddy underfoot. She saw the low branch in time and ducked to pass under it. She got her head under all right, but the branch caught in the hood of her anorak, plucked her neatly off the horse's back and left her suspended like a turkey on a hook, feet nowhere near the ground. For a minute or so she hung there helpless, then, to the joy of every lad who later heard the story, the hood ripped clean off the anorak and she crashed down in a dirty black puddle.

How do I know about this? In woods near racing stables, every tree has its eyes and ears.

THAT'S FUNNY,
I DON'T REMEMBER
THAT TREE BEING
THERE BEFORE

A RACEHORSE'S BEST FRIEND

You know how the human race lets itself be divided up into dog people and cat people. 'Of course,' someone says, 'I love *all* animals' (as if the person they're talking to is either incapable of love or notorious for doing horrible things to his or her pet). 'But,' they continue, 'give me a cat/dog any time.' Then they spill out some old cliché, such as:

'Dogs are so much more *genuine*' or
'Cats are only out for themselves' or
'Cats are so much more *intelligent*'
or, in Ireland,
'A cat/dog is your only man.'

Racehorses are divided in much the same way. It can be a lonely life in the box for up to 22 hours a day, and many a racehorse's best friend is his rabbit, or, more commonly, his goat. Rabbits, though good company, don't have quite as much authority; they sometimes get trodden on by mistake, too, and then the horse needs a new rabbit. Goats have more presence; they will stand quietly all day beside their horse, calming and fortifying him for the races ahead.

Clive Brittain had a horse that liked to relax with a football. Happy Hector, he was called. Clive would throw the ball up, and Happy Hector would nod it back. He got very good at it, even appeared on television.

Of course, Happy Hector regarded his football more as an aid to relaxing from the strains of being a racehorse than as a true companion. He, like many other horses, could still form a relationship with another animal. And often that animal is ... another horse! If you put a group of horses out in a field, there would be a few scuffles, a fight or two, but most would find one special companion to trot round with.

Racehorses, though, don't get out much, and stable life can make them restless. Some become 'boxwalkers', turning this way and that in the narrow space, and in danger of injuring themselves. That's why trainers put in the rabbit, or goat, to soothe them. For horses who prefer horses, one remedy is to make a hole in the wall of the box, and cover it with strong wire, so that the horse can see through into the next box. It's not great, but it's better than 22 hours' solitary!

THEY'RE HAVING YOU ON, LAD,
YOU DON'T HAVE TO EXERCISE
THE GOAT AS WELL.

FUNNY HORSES

Pat McCarron went over to Leopardstown in Ireland to ride in a Champion Hurdle on an English horse. He was due to ride only in the big race, but then an old farmer came up and asked him to ride in a $2\frac{1}{2}$-mile 'chase. Pat politely declined.

'No, I don't want another ride, thank you. I want to get off back to Dublin and catch my plane to London.'

The old farmer went away. Half an hour later he was back.

'Come on,' he said, 'you've got to ride this horse. I'll give you two hundred quid.'

AND YOU'LL HAVE TO SHOUT, HE'S A BIT DEAF AS WELL

Pat hummed and hawed a bit, then decided he'd take it on.

'It's a good ride,' the farmer assured him. 'Nothing wrong with it. Give you a very good ride it will. Good leaper and all.'

In the paddock the farmer met him again. 'Look,' he said, 'this is a great horse. Sure to win. There's only one thing you have to do. When you're coming up to the fences, measure your strides and say: "One, two, up." Always shout "Up" when you want him to take off. You got that? Dig him in the ribs, see your stride, then just as you want him to take off, give him a boot in the belly and shout "Up!"'

Pat thought: 'Jesus, these farmers,' and rode down to the start.

It was a nice type of animal, though. He jumped off well, and soon they were at the first fence. The horse crashed straight through it, not a hint of a leap. Pat was shaken, lucky to have stayed on. But the horse had tailed off; they were well behind.

Pat thought: 'I'd better do what the old boy said.' So, at the next fence, he counted: 'One, two, UP!!' The horse rose like a champion and soared over the fence. So Pat decided to do this at each fence. They went round, and gradually started catching the field. Coming to the second last, Pat could see he was in with a chance. 'One, two, UP!' They hit the front. The horse went on well and came in a winner by ten lengths.

Pat rode into the winner's enclosure, all smiles, but still puzzled about his instructions. He said to the farmer:

'Why did I have to do all that "One, two, UP"? What the hell was all that for?'

'Oh, bejasus, the horse is blind.'

A Strong Sprinter

Warwick. A five-furlong race. I was going down to post. At Warwick you have to go a furlong, pull up and go back down again. We cantered off down. Sprinters are usually a bit strong, and this one felt pretty lively. However, I was just getting him pulled up nicely when John Lowe shot past me.

To my horse this was competition. His ears went back, he took off again and went whizzing past John Lowe. As I went by I yelled:

'You bloody idiot, why don't you pull up? You've set me alight!'

I got my horse slowed down and reasonably under control . . . and John Lowe went past me again!

'Can't help it!' he called, tearing ahead.

Off we set again, up the hill. This time I took my horse in by the brick wall where a tree sticks out. I headed him straight for the tree, holding him in as best I could. We were still motoring a bit, but when he saw the tree – he did the splits! We skidded crazily but I stayed on. At last, I thought, arms round his neck, I've stopped him. Then:

Whooosh! John Lowe again! I could have sworn he had gone. In a flash my horse was after him. I lost an iron as we hurtled after John Lowe. Got the iron back. Past John Lowe again. By now it was total farce, worse than the Keystone Kops. We went the whole way round the course like this; not till we'd gone past the winning post did I get him properly pulled up. I jumped off fast. I'd had enough of that horse for one afternoon. What's more, after suffering all that embarrassment, I then had to go and speak to the owner and trainer – who were Not Amused.

Epitaph

The comedian Sandy Powell had a poem that could be the epitaph of every horse that failed to bring joy to his owner's heart. It went:

> His sire belonged to a milkman
> His dam I've forgotten somehow
> I think he takes after his dam, sir
> 'Cos he's no damn good up to now.

Sandy must be one of the great racing comedians. He had various sporting 'selves', such as Sandy the Goalkeeper and Sandy the Jockey. This was one of the jockey poems:

> Once I rode a Derby winner,
> Rode him at an awful pace,
> Rode him home to get his dinner,
> Couldn't ride him in the race.

> Talk about your leading jockeys,
> I'm the leader of the pack,
> One day I took all the prizes,
> But they made me put them back!

In For a Quick One

At Bath there's a tight bend with a pub on the other side. If you miss that bend, go too wide, the other jockeys will have you after the race. 'Been in for a drink?' they say, as if it could never happen to them.

I had a horse at Bath who was not really a competitive sort, even though I'd spent some time geeing him up on the gallops at home. On race day, I jumped on him in the paddock, looked ahead, and what did I see? Big black blinkers. Strange, I thought, blinkers are for shy horses. I'd never seen this one with blinkers on before. It all seemed out of character.

I took him out, and revved him up a bit. Going down to post he seemed fine; responded well. We got in the stalls, no trouble. Then when he jumped off, he was another horse. He reached 100 mph in about 30 yards and looked capable of more. We came to the famous turn, and didn't. Straight on we charged. What's going to stop him? I thought, hanging on. Fortunately, the rails did. He hit the far rails and the impact bounced him round.

Once he'd been turned, he shot off across the track and clipped the inside rails. He hadn't finished yet. For his next trick he wanted to do a right-handed turn back to the stables.

We went over to the wall, which is off the racecourse, then at a furlong and a half I got him round and back on the track. Not only were we still in the race, we'd been flying so fast we were in second position! After that, though, I didn't press him too hard; getting home alive seemed more important.

The Pontefract Ghost

It was a nice sunny day at Pontefract. The late-afternoon sun beamed over the course, and I was happily out front, having made all the running.

I was on the rails, and turned into the straight, a furlong and a half from home. To my surprise, I thought I could hear something coming up behind me. I turned round and saw a shadow tucked in behind. Right, I thought, we'll get rid of him. I gave my horse a backhander, and asked him for more effort. Again I glanced round; still it was there.

Jesus, I couldn't get rid of it. He's going to beat me! So I gave my horse everything I could think of, we zoomed the last few yards and to my intense relief were first past the post. Now I had time for a real look round. Nothing there! I'd spent a furlong and a half racing my own shadow. We won by fifteen lengths.

IT WAS A PHOTO FINISH —
AND THE SHADOW WON

ORDERS IS ORDERS IS ORDERS

In the paddock the trainer has his last chance to issue instructions to his jockey. Then, after the trainer's finished, the lad takes over and leads you out on the course. Some of them get a bit carried away by the occasion, and seem to forget about what they're doing. Many's the time I've had to break in, just before we're on the course, and say:

'Are you going to canter down with me?'

They look mystified: 'Why? Why?'

'Because you haven't taken the leading rein off!'

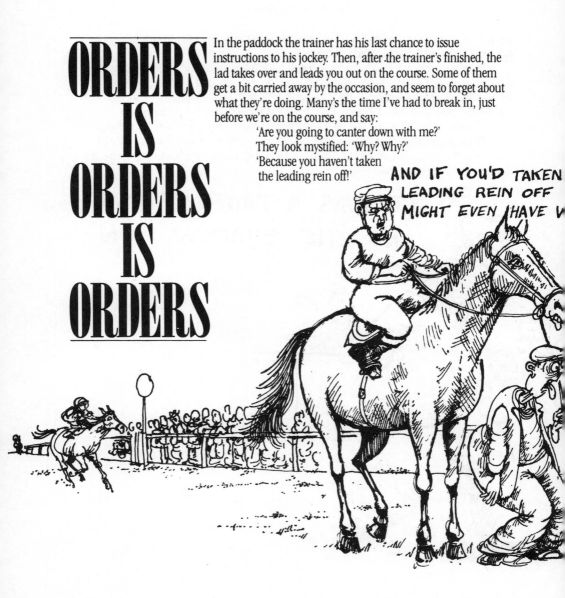

AND IF YOU'D TAKEN LEADING REIN OFF MIGHT EVEN HAVE V

62

Sit and Wait

You can coach apprentices, and you can over-coach them. If they haven't got the experience, there's always the chance they will just be confused.

An apprentice finished a race at Hamilton, only to find that the stewards weren't happy with the way he'd ridden. They had him in.

'Now then, boy. What were your orders?'

'Oh, "Sit and wait", sir.'

The stewards sent the boy out. They conferred, but couldn't decide. They called the boy back together with the trainer, a Mr Cartwright we'll call him.

'Yes, now, son. You were told to sit and wait. But how long did Mr Cartwright tell you to wait?'

'Oh, till Ayr next week, sir!'

Give it a Trip

Mr Cartwright also figures in this next story. A jockey had ridden a horse for him, but it hadn't done brilliantly. After the race, the jockey said to Cartwright:

'You know, really I think it needs a trip. Try giving it a trip.'

To 99.9 per cent of racing men this means to run the horse over a longer distance.

'All right,' said Cartwright. 'Well, thanks very much for riding him. We'll see what we can do.'

The jockey heard no more until, about two months later, he met Cartwright at a meeting and asked him how the horse had got on.

'Oh,' said Cartwright, looking a little glum, 'not very well really. No, it hasn't done much. But,' he went on, brightening, 'I gave it a trip, like you said. I sent it all the way to Hamilton!'

Even the Best-Laid Plans

Jockey, quietly to trainer, while unsaddling in the winner's ring after an unintended victory:

'Sorry, sir, I couldn't do anything about it.'

Trainer, in loud voice: 'Well done, lad. Very well done!'

The jockey weighs in and has just come through the door of the jockey's room when – Wham! He gets a great thwack round the head.

Trainer to jockey: 'And next time, do as you're bleeding well told!'

A Crafty Move

When the jockey is deaf, the trainer's problems are suddenly multiplied.
   'Look, go easy on him, Bill,' says the trainer quietly, 'he's not quite ready.'
Bill, though, is not only deaf, he doesn't care!
'What,' he roars, 'do you want me to stop him?'

On Sandown Hill

The central character in this story is trainer Michael Jarvis's new Mercedes. I'd gone for a day's racing at Sandown, got there early and parked my car in the front row at the top of the hill. I got out to talk to someone, locked the car, gave the keys to my companion, who went off, and then started chatting to this other feller.

   While we were talking, we were spotted by an old character called Chick who goes round the racecourses. Chick was always one to ask for a snippet of information, and true to form he started climbing the hill towards us. Traffic was coming steadily on to the course and beginning to park below us.

   Puffing and wheezing, Chick at last reached the summit. He greeted us and leant on the car to take a moment's rest. His weight was enough to set the car moving ... and it began to roll down the hill. With no keys I couldn't get inside, so there I was suddenly pushing like mad against the windscreen to try and stop it. No good. Others rushed to help but it was too late. The car had found its own momentum and was not to be resisted. It had gone thirty yards and was gathering speed ....

   Down at the bottom of the hill Michael Jarvis had parked his brand-new Mercedes. It was a rather special occasion, and his wife and daughters had come with him for a day out in the gleaming new car.

Michael Jarvis and family were stretching their legs in the sunshine beside the new car, walking round it, beginning to think about the pleasures of lunch … when they heard shouts, coming from further up the hill. They looked up, to see a super-agitated Willie Carson chasing a big black car that was heading straight for them!

The Jarvises skipped out of the way just in time and my car thwacked into the back wing of the new Mercedes, just by the petrol tank. Then it rasped a passage all the way down one side and came to a stop by the front wheel. What a mess. Two new doors and two new panels – and all before the first race! Is that a nice way to treat a trainer?

You'd think it would be impossible for a jockey to get on the wrong horse. Well, I almost made it, one day at Stockton. The source of my troubles was a green saddle which I'd bought from an Australian jockey, Lance Harvey. I don't really like the colour green – I'd never seen a green saddle before – but the design of it appealed, so I bought it.

I came out to the paddock at Stockton to get my orders, and saw my green saddle going round. The bell rang for the jockeys to mount, so I went to get on my horse. At the time I thought it was a bit funny that the trainer didn't follow me over, but I carried on, reached the horse, got hold of the reins. The lad, who was holding him, gave me a pained sort of look. I put my leg up, for him to help me into the saddle. He didn't move.

Come on, I thought, what's the matter with you? But the lad wasn't at all keen to throw me up. He just stood there, as if he'd forgotten how to speak. Someone, at last, said:

'That's not your horse.'

'What d'ya mean? Here's my saddle on it. The only green saddle on the course.'

'Yes, Willie,' said my helper, gently. 'But you're not using this saddle in this race. You're using *that* saddle over *there*.'

He pointed across the paddock to the only other riderless horse. On its back I recognized my heavy brown saddle. Feeling like a cross between a three-year-old child and a lunatic on one of his rave days, I allowed myself to be led across.

What had happened was, my good valet had decided to loan the green saddle to another jockey, but without asking me. I, meanwhile, had gone out to the paddock forgetting that I should be using my heaviest saddle for that race. I'd looked up, seen the green saddle on the other jockey's horse, and . . . that's right, you've got it. And a helluva sight quicker than I did!

The Horse That Wasn't

If there's anything worse than trying to get on another jockey's horse, it's looking for a horse that isn't there at all! It was mid-summer, I'd been riding in day and night meetings, usually with a ride in each race. So here we were one evening at Newmarket, after six races during the day at Goodwood. There were seven races on the card instead of the usual six. Maybe that was what threw me: I knew I had six rides, so may have assumed subconsciously that there were only six races. Anyway, I was feeling fine, well in the groove. Each race, put the colours on, jump on the scales, bell goes, helmet on, tie the hat, grab the stick, out the door and off to the paddock.

In the paddock again. I was wearing Lady Beaverbrook's colours and expecting to ride for trainer Dick Hern over one mile and six furlongs. Everyone else in the paddock was preparing for a seven-furlong race, but for the time being they were in their world and I was in mine. As I walked in, I recognized Robert Armstrong's paddock sheet on a familiar-looking horse. I'd ridden that horse before. Strange, I thought, *that* horse in *this* race. As I walked past Robert Armstrong, I said:

'Funny distance to be running your filly.'

Armstrong looked back at me, an odd expression on his face. He sort of smiled, but didn't say anything. I went further on, then stood and waited. The other jockeys came in, and started chatting away with their trainers. Time passed. The other horses were going round, but where was mine? I began to think they must have had trouble tacking him up; still he didn't come into the paddock. I heard a few cackles in the crowd. After a bit I looked up at the board; my name wasn't there.

I thought: how do I get out of this one? There I was, standing in the paddock with Lady Beaverbrook's colours on. Somehow it had got into my head that I was riding her horse in the sixth race; in fact I didn't have a ride at all! What to do but brazen it out? I mounted an invisible hobbyhorse and whipped myself out of the paddock as fast as I could.

Horseless before the start. It's not been done a lot. Why does it have to happen to me?

70

DEMONOLOGY

A British folklorist once wrote: 'Living superstitions are much more numerous today than is sometimes supposed, nor are they found only among the foolish or uneducated.'

IT'S SUCH A COINCIDENCE, US BOTH HAVING THE SAME SUPERSTITION, SO I'LL OVERLOOK YOUR ERRATIC DRIVING

Quite so. Why, even jockeys have their little rites to keep um bad spirits away.

I always put my right boot on first. Start right, be right all day, that's the theory. There are many superstitions like it – dressing in a certain order, using the peg nearest the door, leaving the room last, pulling an ear, wearing 'lucky' underpants until they are in shreds, then wearing them under another pair. Different jockeys, different habits. One of the most superstitious jockeys was Harry Carr. Some of his rituals were amazing.

Once, on his way to the races, he saw a skewbald pony in a field. When this happened, Harry had to get hold of his right toe with his left hand and hold it until he saw another four-legged animal. That's not so outrageous, you may say. No, except that Harry was driving his car at 70 mph when the skewbald appeared, and refused to stop and let anyone else drive!

All new things have to be broken in, and new colours are no exception. If you are starting with a new owner and put new colours on, straight from the valet, you're sure to get dropped by the horse. So I always take the precaution of throwing any new set of colours on the floor and stamping on them. That way, the colours are already dirty and there's no reason to fall off the horse and get them dirty the hard way. Logical, really.

I also had a lucky blue suit. I didn't wear it all that often, but every time there was a big occasion, out came the blue suit, and things seemed to go well. Trouble is, you can overwork a suit. It started to shine. You can sit on the shiniest part and hope to get away with it for a while; then it started to go in other places. No-one actually said anything, no 'Tramps Ball again, tonight, Willie?' but in the end I had to go down to the tailor, choose some cloth, get measured up for a replacement suit, try it on, throw it on the floor, stamp on it . . . .

GET ME TO THE TRACK ON TIME

Many of the biggest races in a jockey's career aren't seen by the public at all. This is because they aren't performed at race tracks but on roads leading to them. With night meetings following close on the heels of day meetings, drastic feats are needed.

For instance, what do you do when you're in the last race at Goodwood, starting at 4.35, and then down to ride in the 6.15 at Newmarket, 115 miles away as the crow flies, a good bit longer by road, and with London in between? And for 6.15 read 5.55, as jockeys have to be present at least 20 minutes before a race. Here's what you do.

You fix a police escort to get you clear of Goodwood. You canter rather than walk your last ride – by chance a winner – into the winner's enclosure. You get someone called Clive Brittain

THAT'S RIGHT, I'M THE ONE THAT DISAPPEARED LAST YEAR

(or a stable lad if you can find one) to hang on to the horse. Saddle off, weigh in. Seize jacket and coat, rush down to the car. To liven things up Clive Brittain, who is running behind you through the departing masses, shouts:

'Catch that man! He's a thief! Catch him!'

You elude would-be captors, dive into the car, start up, belt down outside the line of cars, police escort's siren now wailing. Cars coming the other way swerve to avoid you; the driver of a huge sludge wagon advancing up the hill appears to have a heart attack as he sees you heading for him, and veers off into a pine wood. You never see him again (has anyone seen him again?) but at last you complete the mile and a half to Goodwood airfield. A light plane is waiting, engines running.

You rise into the air, look down at vanishing Goodwood, catch your breath for a few seconds. What are you, an international acrobat, a jetsetter (God forbid), why do you do all this? Perhaps in real life you are a Beaujolais shipper delivering the latest vintage? No, you are a jock, and the plane is already descending to land in a Suffolk field.

Action again. Into another car, zoom to race course – and get there at 5.45. This is not only 10 minutes early, it's ahead of the other bunch of jocks flying over from Goodwood who, may they rot for it, had refused to wait for you and let you share their plane because you, unlike them, were in the last race and they had thought that was too risky!

All Stood Up

Another way to be sure of catching the plane to Newmarket is . . . don't ride in the last race! It was a bit late in the order of events when this answer to his problems was suddenly forced on Eph, but then, he didn't really have much choice. There he was, down at the start, with the last plane for the evening meeting at Newmarket due to leave in minutes. If he didn't catch it, there'd be hell to pay the other end.

Meanwhile, the horse beneath him was being a very awkward animal. It gave no sign of appreciating Eph's difficulties; rather the opposite, it was extremely reluctant to line up with the others.

The starter watched as Eph and his wayward horse twirled and gavotted in a very unmerry manner, yards back from the tapes. They looked a hopeless case, so, when he reckoned he had waited long enough, the starter let the other runners go.

That was it. Eph was left at the start. Not only that, the horse still refused to turn and be ridden back. Drastic steps were needed if Eph was to catch his plane. But how to do it? Just as captive airmen didn't get out of Stalag Luft III in one bound, so jockeys don't find it easy to evaporate at race meetings. Eph decided that bluff was the only way.

Quietly he beckoned over the whipper-in.

'Hold his head, will you.'

The whipper-in, bless his trusting soul, obeyed. Eph, in a blur of light, dismounted and removed his saddle. To the now-startled whipper-in, he said:

'Hold him like that, will you. Got to have a word.'

By now the starter had come down his steps and was heading towards his car. Suddenly a small man carrying a saddle stepped into his path.

'Give us a lift back, sir?' said Eph.

They got in the starter's car and drove down to the finish. Eph sprinted to collect his clothes, and caught the plane with seconds to spare. Only when they were in the air did he dare look back towards the start. But the view from his window gave him only the quickest

glimpse of that part of the course, and he
spotted neither horse nor whipper-in,
though presumably they were still out
there somewhere. Perhaps, thought Eph,
turning to face forward in his seat, he
would hear of them tomorrow.

Riders in the Sky

Although aircraft have their attractions, they are a terrible expense and not the kind of transport a jockey can freely resort to out of his own pocket. So, within the UK, we mostly travel by road. Before looking some more at that part of our lives – the squealing tyres, police sirens, etc – it should be said that no car is likely to help anyone match Paul Cook's current record of riding at three race meetings in one day. Courtesy of his sheikh-owner's helicopter, Paul did the rounds of Sandown Park, Bath and Nottingham, and lived to tell the tale.

Perhaps one day the sky will be full of one-man helicopters, piloted by small figures in peaked caps and riding boots, a saddle over the knee as they dart from one venue to the next. Perhaps.

I'M GOING TO HAVE TO LEAVE STRAIGHT AFTER THIS RACE

Dog One

Meanwhile, back on the road. The *Sunday Times* magazine had asked me to take part in their 'Life In The Day Of' series. Brough Scott was to write it, and he and Gerry Cranham the photographer came over. We started early in the morning with riding-work, then went and had breakfast; photographs were taken, I got changed and we took a plane up from Newbury to Doncaster, where I had a meeting.

The plane was a little bit late, but we landed safely and got in a taxi. We were getting a bit concerned about the time, so we asked the driver if he'd hurry up. He obliged, the taxi whizzed off and things were looking just about OK. Then, on the outskirts of Doncaster, the taxi punctured. I looked at the code sign for the taxi: it said 'DOG ONE'. Yes, I thought, a right dog we've got here! And missed my ride in the first race.

One way and another it was a great Life In The Day. I didn't ride a winner. Nothing happened at Doncaster, then we flew down to Wolverhampton for an evening meeting and I didn't get a win there either, despite having one highly fancied horse. I prefer to blame it on the taxi – Dog One, by name and nature!

Motorway policeman to jockey after 20-mile chase: 'Ere, didn't you know I've been trying to catch you?'
Jockey, through window: 'Yes, but didn't I give you a good run?'

Midlands Express

To Wolverhampton. In the back seat, jockeys Frank Durr and Greville Starkey. At the wheel, my racing secretary and chauffeur, Ted. Just the three of them. I had been riding at a day meeting and was flying up to Wolverhampton for the evening's races. Ted was to meet me there and drive me back to Newmarket. They were a bit behind the clock, thanks to the two in the back who earlier had insisted on a prolonged stop at a pub where they knew the landlord. They came to some roadworks and a feller in the road with a Stop/Go sign. He was peering at people and letting them through in small packets. 'Stop' if I don't like you, 'Go' if I do; that kind of thing.

From the back seat, with laughter: 'It's "Stop". Stop! It's "Go". No, he's got "Stop". He's got "Go". Go!

Ted decided he'd had enough. He got up speed and tore past the Stop-Go man. The wind from the car sent his sign spinning like a catherine wheel.

Chanting from the back seat: 'He's swallowed his flag! He's swallowed his flag!'

Ted thought: 'I'll cool you two down as well. First you make me late, then you sit in the back, jumping up and down and giggling all the time.'

They closed on Wolverhampton, still late. Their way was blocked by a queue of cars on the bridge before the first right-turn to the track. Ted, reasoning that there was unlikely to be any traffic coming off the track since the meeting was about to begin, shot down the outside of the queue, turned right and whizzed the wrong way up the one-way system to the track.

Ted stopped the car, and looked in the back. No-one there. Had they jumped out? He looked over the back of the seat and found both jockeys, panic-struck, burying themselves in the floor.

I was already in the weighing room when Durr and Starkey entered, trembling.

'That Ted,' they said, quivering with fright. 'He's mad. He's mad.' Followed by the dark warning: 'He'll kill you!'

Well, he hasn't yet!

Düsseldorf

Travelling abroad to ride, easy enough with a group, has its problems when you go there on your own. I had a Sunday date at Düsseldorf, so I flew out there in the morning, cleared Customs and waited in the hall for someone to meet me. No-one came, the sun was shining, I was a little impatient to be going somewhere, so I walked out to the line of taxis.

'Rennenbahn,' I said to the driver, expending in one burst twenty per cent of my stock of German words.

The driver grunted. We set off. Twenty minutes later, we drew alongside the familiar sight of a racing stadium. I paid the driver, got out; he drove away.

As I stood alone on the pavement, it struck me that everything was very quiet for a race day, even if the meeting wasn't due to start for a few hours. I looked again. Gates were shut that shouldn't be. With dawning panic it occurred to me that this was not the place; that Düsseldorf, a city of 700,000 inhabitants in the middle of the Ruhr, has more than one racetrack. Worse, it has four! Ted, my racing secretary, had made the booking and I, not so cleverly, had assumed I would be riding at the track called Düsseldorf.

So where should I have been? Up on the corner I saw a hotel. Time was passing. I began to walk towards the hotel. By the time I got there I was running. Sweating as well, from lugging a full bag of kit including a saddle. I went inside. There was no-one there either.

Yes, at last someone came. Someone spoke English. A newspaper was found; turn to the sports page, scan the runners and riders.

'There I am!' I cry at last, seeing my name.

'Where, please?'

'There!'

'Ach. Ja. No. But it's not right.'

'What do you mean, it's not right?'

'It's not here. This Düsseldorf, that Bremen. Is *weiter*, you know. WEITER. Furzer.' Waving of hands towards heaven.

'I must get there.'

A taxi came. I got in.

'Rennenbahn?' said the driver, a different driver, without the ghost of a smile.

'Ja,' I said.

I arrived in a reasonably calm state at the track, where my hosts were dancing about in a highly nervous condition. Word had already reached them from their airport man, who had missed me, that I wasn't on the plane.

'What happened? What happened?' they wanted to know.

'I came by taxi.'

'Oh, you came by taxi?'

'Yes. Well, two taxis, really.'

'Vot?'

You don't see so many of the old racetrack characters about today. There was a time, not long ago, when a regular crowd of them would converge on meetings. How they got there, and where they came from, was their own affair; the one principle they stuck to was – don't pay for anything.

The great aim of it all was to earn a few bob for leading up the horses. For that they had to get into the paddock – and without paying. The dodge was to have a bucket and sponge. So long as they carried a bucket and sponge, they thought they were all right. Darkie Hinds was one of the great experts. He'd carry his bucket and sponge up to the entrance to the paddock and mumble a trainer's name to the gateman.

'OK. Pass,' the gateman would say, and he'd be in. Then he'd shuffle round collecting lead-ups for ten bob a go. Not bad for the outlay on an old bucket and sponge. Sometimes not even that. One day Darkie got into the paddock with a bucket he'd nicked off someone's rhubarb. It had no bottom to it, but what the hell, reasoned Darkie. It wasn't meant for horses, it was meant to pacify those bloody interfering gatemen!

ARE YOU READY?

Starting stalls have taken some of the excitement out of racing since they were introduced a dozen years back. Now there's not much for the jockey to do at the start – except maybe distract a rival and get him looking sideways when the stall opens! Otherwise, starting is very much down to the horses; they are trained to jump away, and there's not a lot more to it.

In the old days the jockeys had more scope. They were more critical, too, of the starters. As Charlie Smirke said one day, after noticing that the finishing judge wore glasses and the starter had sunglasses on: 'We've got no ruddy chance today, jocks. They're blind at both ends!'

There was an art in coming up to the old-fashioned gate at just the right moment. And it wasn't beyond the odd jockey to try and con the starter.

'No sir! No sir!' he'd cry anxiously, as he manoeuvred for position. 'No sir! No sir!' Then, noticing that someone else was not quite ready, he'd suddenly shout *Right*, sir!' and hope this would jolt the starter into letting them go.

One jockey, now retired, seemed to live a charmed life as far as certain starters were concerned. When the other jockeys were all up on the tapes, he'd suddenly wheel away, confident that the starter wouldn't let the others go without him. Then he'd turn, come trotting back, and as soon as he reached the line, the starter almost invariably let them go. He, of course, jumped away, but the others were left flat-footed.

Not that it was generally safe to assume that the starter would wait if you wheeled away. Many's the jockey who's been left facing the wrong way, either because he or the horse picked the wrong moment, or because the starter didn't react as he might have done. I got left at Pontefract one day, at the start of a six-furlong race. There I was, riding the odds-on favourite. My horse wheeled away, then the others all lined up and went! When I turned and saw what had happened, I couldn't believe my eyes. The starter was shocked, too. When he saw me there, he just boggled, mouth open. He hadn't seen me because I'd got hidden from his view in a space behind his car which was pulled up to the rails. It was too late to recall the others, but you could see the horror all over his face. My God! I've dumped the favourite!

Fighting Fit

You'd also find horses who were so keen, they'd want to take on the tapes as well, and beat them! A friend of mine rode a horse at Phoenix Park which must have been doped to the eyeballs. The favourite was very unsettled and kept whipping round, so the starter wouldn't let them go. Meanwhile, the doped horse brewed and fumed, until it could stand waiting no longer. So it took off – straight into the gate. Usually the tapes would break, but not this time. The jockey went sliding up them, catching his throat a terrible jar. He said afterwards: 'If that's what it's like to be hanged, I'm glad they've abolished it!'

At Doncaster one gloomy afternoon, I was riding one of these gate-busters. At first he was entirely placid, no trouble. As we lined up, I just gave him a gentle message, then Whaaam! Away he went. We went off so fast, I was sure we'd broken the gate. Then, what seemed like a furlong later, Whaaang! I was catapulting backwards. Sky, grass, sky, grass, sky, grass, sky, grass ... I ended up behind the rest of the field!

On other occasions you'd get a terrible tangle when one side of the gate mechanism worked, and the other side jammed. So the gate would go up lopsided, half the field getting away and the other half still on the line and screaming for release. Mostly the starter would recall – though not always.

Self-Starters

From time to time you'd come across a horse who'd got the tapes worked out better than the jockeys. In Ireland there was an old chaser called Maybird. Chasers only have the one starting string to deal with, and Maybird's trick was to catch hold of it with her teeth. She'd give it a pull to release the spring, up went the tape and Maybird was away!

Another horse, Le Garçon d'Or, used to move forward until he could put his nose against the tape. Then he'd stand there, waiting. As soon as the tape moved, the jockey had to duck; usually this was Alec Russell, who knew what to expect, but anyone else stood to get a nasty shock! Still, it worked for the horse. He's in the record books for winning 33 races; what does it matter if he left a few headless jockeys along the way?

Blackout Parade

An Irish trainer had a horse that wouldn't line up with the others. So he rigged up a pair of blinkers with blinds that fitted over the holes. A pair of strings ran back behind the horse's ears and the idea was, when the tapes went up, the jockey pulled on the strings and raised the blinds. First time out, the jockey pulled the strings and the horse jumped off with the others. But what the jockey didn't know was that the little blinds inside the blinkers hadn't come up at all. He only found out when they ran straight into the first hurdle!

Powell's Passage was another: a big grey horse, a bit troublesome. He always had to

IT'S USUALLY THE HORSE THAT'S NERVOUS ABOUT GOING INTO THE STALLS

have a blind, a black hood, over his head to get him into the stalls. On one **occasion** we had a starter who always liked to get us away as soon as he could. The problem was, Powell's Passage was such a big horse, with such a great long neck on him, that when the starter opened the gates, I was still straining forward to reach the blind and remove it.

The horse jumped out when the gates opened, but that was all he could do. We took no further part. He was the favourite, too. Explain that to the stewards!

They're Off! No, He's Off!

At Leicester the starter was renowned for his fixed routine. He'd walk slowly towards his ladder, and begin climbing it, step by step, in a very deliberate way. Then, while everyone waited, he'd dash up the last two steps and grab the handle that worked the gate. That way, he reckoned, he'd avoid any funny tricks and get a better start.

One drizzly wet day, this starter launched into his final sprint. He got up one step, then slipped. To try and save himself he grabbed for the starting handle, but missed.

Down below, the jockeys, well aware of his tactics, were poised to go. And, when they saw the starter's flailing hand descend, they went. As they surged forward the tapes failed to rise, and the weight of horses and men brought the whole gate down.

In the ordinary way this would have been a false start, with the runners recalled. Unfortunately, the starter was now lying flat on his back and couldn't get his red flag up to make the necessary signal. A furlong away the false-start man, whose job it was to stop the runners and send them back, could see that some horses and riders were still threshing about in the tangle at the gate, but no red flag was to be seen. The surviving horses thundered past him, their jockeys not knowing if they were in a race or not. On they flew, round the bend, disappearing into the mists of one of the most frantic stewards' inquiries ever seen at the Leicester course!

IF YOU ASK ME, THAT SHOULD HAVE BEEN A FALSE START